LIA CHANG

DEREK WALCOTT

White Egrets

Derek Walcott was born in St. Lucia in 1930. He is the author of eight collections of plays and a book of essays. He received the Nobel Prize in Literature in 1992. *White Egrets* is his fourteenth collection of poems.

Plays

Dream on Monkey Mountain and Other Plays

The Joker of Seville and O Babylon!

Remembrance and Pantomime

Three Plays: The Last Carnival; Beef, No Chicken; Branch of the Blue Nile

The Odyssey

The Haitian Trilogy

Walker and The Ghost Dance

Poems

In a Green Night: Poems 1948–1960

The Castaway and Other Poems

The Gulf and Other Poems

Another Life

Sea Grapes

The Star-Apple Kingdom

The Fortunate Traveller

Midsummer

Collected Poems: 1948–1984

The Arkansas Testament

Omeros

The Bounty

Tiepolo's Hound

The Prodigal

Selected Poems

Essays

What the Twilight Says

White Egrets

White Egrets

Poems

DEREK WALCOTT

FARRAR, STRAUS AND GIROUX

NEW YORK

FARRAR, STRAUS AND GIROUX
18 West 18th Street, New York 10011

Distributed in Canada by D&M Publishers, Inc.
Printed in the United States of America
Published in 2010 by Farrar, Straus and Giroux
First paperback edition, 2011

Some of these poems originally appeared, in slightly different form,
in *The Atlantic, Believer, Epiphany, The Georgia Review, Granta, Little
Star, The New Yorker, The New York Review of Books, Orion*, and
A Public Space.

The Library of Congress has cataloged the hardcover edition
as follows:
Walcott, Derek.
       White egrets : poems / Derek Walcott. — 1st ed.
          p.   cm.
       ISBN 978-0-374-28929-4 (hardcover : alk. paper)
       I. Title.

   PR9272.9.W3W49 2010
   811'.54—dc22

                                                    2009031895

Paperback ISBN: 978-0-374-53270-3

Designed and composed by Gretchen Achilles/Wavetrap Design

www.fsgbooks.com

10   9   8   7   6   5   4   3   2   1

For Stephanos, Matteo, Bobby, Vanni, Caz and Glyn

White Egrets

1.

The chessmen are as rigid on their chessboard
as those life-sized terra-cotta warriors whose vows
to their emperor with bridle, shield and sword
were sworn by a chorus that has lost its voice;
no echo in that astonishing excavation.
Each soldier gave an oath, each gave his word
to die for his emperor, his clan, his nation,
to become a chess piece, breathlessly erect
in shade or crossing sunlight, without hours—
from clay to clay and odourlessly strict.
If vows were visible they might see ours
as changeless chessmen in the changing light
on the lawn outside where bannered breakers toss
and the palms gust with music that is time's
above the chessmen's silence. Motion brings loss.
A sable blackbird twitters in the limes.

2.

Your two cats squat, heraldic sphinxes, with such
desert indifference, such "who-the-hell-are-you?" calm,
they rise and stride away leisurely from your touch,
waiting for you only. To be cradled in one arm,
belly turned upward to be stroked by a brush
tugging burrs from their fur, eyes slitted
in ecstasy. The January sun spreads its balm
on earth's upturned belly, shadows that have always fitted
their shapes, re-fit them. Breakers spread welcome.
Accept it. Watch how spray will burst
like a cat scrambling up the side of a wall,
gripping, sliding, surrendering; how, at first,
its claws hook then slip with a quickening fall
to the lace-rocked foam. That is the heart, coming home,
trying to fasten on everything it moved from,
how salted things only increase its thirst.

3.

This was my early war, the bellowing quarrels,
at the pitch of noon, of men moving cargoes
while gulls screeched their monotonous vowels
in complex curses without coming to blows;
muscular men swirling codfish barrels
and heaving rice bags, who had stunted nicknames,
who could, one-handed, hoist phenomenal rolls
of wire, hoist flapping galvanize with both arms
to pitch it into the hold while hooks and winches
swung nearby. At lunch they ate in the shade
of mountainous freight bound with knots and cinches,
ignoring the gulls with their boulders of bread.
Then one would be terribly injured, one lose a leg
to rum and diabetes. You would watch him shrink
into his nickname, not too proud to beg,
who would roar like a lorry revving in the prime of his drink.

4.

White Egrets

I

Cautious of time's light and how often it will allow
the morning shadows to lengthen across the lawn
the stalking egrets to wriggle their beaks and swallow
when you, not they, or you and they, are gone;
for clattering parrots to launch their fleet at sunrise
for April to ignite the African violet
in the drumming world that dampens your tired eyes
behind two clouding lenses, sunrise, sunset,
the quiet ravages of diabetes.
Accept it all with level sentences,
with sculpted settlement that sets each stanza;
learn how the bright lawn puts up no defences
against the egret's stabbing questions and the night's answer.

II

The elegance of those white, orange-billed egrets,
each like a stalking ewer, the thick olive trees,
cedars consoling a stream that roars torrentially
in the wet season; into that peace
beyond desires and beyond regrets,
at which I may arrive eventually,
whose palms droop in the sun like palanquins
with tigerish shadows under them. They shall
be there after my shadow passes with all its sins

into a green thicket of oblivion,
with the rising and setting of a hundred suns
over Santa Cruz Valley when I loved in vain.

III

I watch the huge trees tossing at the edge of the lawn
like a heaving sea without crests, the bamboos plunge
their necks like roped horses as yellow leaves, torn
from the whipping branches, turn to an avalanche;
all this before the rain scarily pours from the burst,
sodden canvas of the sky like a hopeless sail,
gusting in sheets and hazing the hills completely
as if the whole valley were a hull outriding the gale
and the woods were not trees but waves of a running sea.
When light cracks and thunder groans as if cursed
and you are safe in a dark house deep in Santa
Cruz, with the lights out, the current suddenly gone,
you think: "Who'll house the shivering hawk, and the
impeccable egret and the cloud-coloured heron,
and the parrots who panic at the false fire of dawn?"

IV

These birds keep modelling for Audubon,
the Snowy Egret or White Heron in a book
that, in my youth, would open like a lawn
in emerald Santa Cruz, knowing how well they look,
strutting perfection. They speckle the islands
on river-bank, in mangrove marsh or cattle pasture,

gliding over ponds, then balancing on the ridge
of a silken heifer, or fleeing disaster
in hurricane weather, and picking ticks
with their electric stab as if it were sheer privilege
to study them in their mythical conceit
that they have beat across the sea from Egypt
with the pharaonic ibis, its orange beak and feet
profiled in quiet to adorn a crypt,
then launch themselves with wings that, beating faster,
are certain as a seraph's when they beat.

V

The perpetual ideal is astonishment.
The cool green lawn, the quiet trees, the forest
on the hill there, then, the white gasp of an egret sent
sailing into the frame then teetering to rest
with its gawky stride, erect, an egret-emblem!
Another thought surprises: a hawk on the wrist
of a branch, soundlessly, like a falcon,
shoots into heaven, circling above praise or blame,
with the same high indifference as yours,
now dropping to tear a field mouse with its claws.
The page of the lawn and this open page are the same,
an egret astonishes the page, the high hawk caws
over a dead thing, a love that was pure punishment.

VI

I hadn't seen them for half of the Christmas week,
the egrets, and no one told me why they had gone,
but they are back with the rain now, orange beak,
pink shanks and stabbing head, back on the lawn
where they used to be in the clear, limitless rain
of the Santa Cruz Valley, which, when it rains, falls
steadily against the cedars till it mists the plain.
The egrets are the colour of waterfalls,
and of clouds. Some friends, the few I have left,
are dying, but the egrets stalk through the rain
as if nothing mortal can affect them, or they lift
like abrupt angels, sail, then settle again.
Sometimes the hills themselves disappear
like friends, slowly, but I am happier
that they have come back now, like memory, like prayer.

VII

With the leisure of a leaf falling in the forest,
pale yellow spinning against green—my ending.
Soon it will be the dry season, the hills will rust,
the egrets dip their necks undulant, bending,
stabbing at worms and grubs after the rain;
sometimes erect as bowling pins, they stand
as strips of cotton-wool peel from the mountain;
then when they move, gawkily, they move this hand
with their feet's splayed fingers, their darting necks.
We share one instinct, that ravenous feeding
my pen's beak, plucking up wriggling insects

like nouns and gulping them, the nib reading
as it writes, shaking off angrily what its beak rejects.
Selection is what the egrets teach
on the wide open lawn, heads nodding as they read
in purposeful silence, a language beyond speech.

VIII

We were by the pool of a friend's house in St. Croix
and Joseph and I were talking; he stopped the talk,
on this visit I had hoped that he would enjoy,
to point out, with a gasp, not still or stalking
but fixed in the great fruit tree, a sight that shook him
"like something out of Bosch," he said. The huge bird was
suddenly there, perhaps the same one that took him,
a sepulchral egret or heron; the unutterable word was
always with us, like Eumaeus, a third companion
and what got him, who loved snow, what brought it on,
was that the bird was such a spectral white.
Now when at noon or evening on the lawn
the egrets soar together in noiseless flight
or tack, like a regatta, the sea-green grass,
they are seraphic souls, as Joseph was.

5.

The Acacia Trees

I

You used to be able to drive (though I don't) across
the wide, pool-sheeted pasture below the house
to the hot, empty beach and park in the starved shade
of the acacias that print those tiny yellow flowers
(blank, printless beaches are part of my trade);
then there were men with tapes and theodolites who measured
the wild, uneven ground. I watched the doomed acres
where yet another luxury hotel will be built
with ordinary people fenced out. The new makers
of our history profit without guilt
and are, in fact, prophets of a policy
that will make the island a mall, and the breakers
grin like waiters, like taxi drivers, these new plantations
by the sea; a slavery without chains, with no blood spilt—
just chain-link fences and signs, the new degradations.
I felt such freedom writing under the acacias.

II

Bossman, if you look in those bush there, you'll find
a whole set of passport, wallet, I.D., credit card,
that is no use to them, is money on their mind
and is not every time you'll find them afterwards.
You jest leave your bag wif these things on the sand,
and faster than wind they jump out of the bush

while you there swimming and rubbing tanning lotion,
and when you find out it is no good to send
the Special Unit, they done reach Massade.
But I not in that, not me, I does make a lickle
change selling and blowing conch shells, is sad
but is true. Dem faster than any vehicle,
and I self never get in any commotion
except with the waves, and soon all that will be lost.
Is too much tourist and too lickle employment.
How about a lickle life there? Thanks, but Boss,
don't let what I say spoil your enjoyment.

III

You see those breakers coming around Pigeon Island
bowing like nuns in a procession? One thing I know,
when you're gone like my other friends, not to Thailand
or Russia, but wherever it is loved friends go
with their different beliefs, who were like a flock
of seagulls leaving the mirror of the sand,
or a bittern passing lonely Barrel of Beef,
or the sails that an egret hoists leaving its rock;
I go down to the same sea by another road
with manchineel shadows and stunted sea grapes
dwarfed by the wind. I carry something to read:
the wind is bright and shadows race like grief,
I open their books and see their distant shapes
approaching and always arriving, their voices heard
in the page of a cloud, like the soft surf in my head.

6.

For August Wilson

August, the quarter-moon dangles like a bugle
over the brick cantonments of the Morne
whose barrack apartments have the serial glow
of postage stamps; the clouds' letters are torn,
and your sweet instrument is put away as
your silver cornet lies in its velvet case
with all those riffs and arias whose characters argue
the way that wind elates the acacias
until they wrestle with the roar of torrents,
black, jagged silhouettes ready to do battle
with enormous hands and eyes with the coming day
in the brick thickets of Pittsburgh and Seattle,
in plays that are their own battle cry and anthem.
I unhook the quarter-moon to blow their praises,
you, Horace Pippin, Romare, Jacob Lawrence,
I saw the moon's bugle there and thought of them.

7.

For Oliver Jackman

It's what others do, not us, die, even the closest
on a vainglorious, glorious morning, as the song goes,
the yellow or golden palms glorious and all the rest
a sparkling splendour, die. They're practising calypsos,
they're putting up and pulling down tents, vendors are slicing
the heads of coconuts around the Savannah, men
are leaning on, then leaping into pirogues, a moon will be rising
tonight in the same place over Morne Coco, then
the full grief will hit me and my heart will toss
like a horse's head or a threshing bamboo grove
that even you could be part of the increasing loss
that is the daily dial of the revolving shade. Love
lies underneath it all though, the more surprising
the death, the deeper the love, the tougher the life.
The pain is over, feathers close your eyelids, Oliver.
What a happy friend and what a fine wife!
Your death is like our friendship beginning over.

8.

Sicilian Suite

I

Like a blackbird that shot out of the daylight
into the benign gloom of the studio, butting the glass,
fluttering and darting then thudding it again,
as if it were searching for a cage that calms
like my mind with its pitiful searching for an exit
from itself, and thinking these days of Pavese,
of a flight from you (who would have thought your shadow
could have been so solid?), that I would easily
like the trapped bird keep butting the wall of your forehead,
till you let me fly through the window of your gaze
past Pigeon Island to Isola (to sacred Sicily)
from the opening parenthesis of your palms.

II

I am haunted by hedges of pink oleander
along the Sicilian roads, their consonants of gravel
under the tires, by stone piles, by walls whose wonder
is that there was no need to travel
this far, to recognize things I already knew,
except, and now it grows, the odd broken castle
through whose doors peered a Caribbean blue,
and the name Ortigia that rings like crystal
in its fragile balance. In the pine's rustle
and the silver alder's and the olive's, a difference began,

sounds that needed translation. The sea was the same
except for its history. The island was our patron saint's
birthplace. They shared the same name:
Lucia. The heat had the identical innocence
of an island afternoon, but with a difference,
the way the oleanders looked and the olive's green flame.

III

Soothe me, Vittorio, calm me, Quasimodo,
bless me with your clasped palms, cypress, and syllables
of the trimmed orange oleander on Somebody Street.
Screech my pain, starlings, from the stone balcony
that faces the Saracen coast, blind me, Santa Lucia,
patron saint of both isles and eyes, for my lack of vision!
There was a prophecy repeated in her smallest gestures
to the madness of an old man who loved a brown faun
that grazed on his heart even in drought.
All of you, save him! Save his clogged heart
like a tree thick with prayers like the starlings
repeating their verses from the barred windows
of Passeggio Adorno, vowing a new start
as he watches the transients hunched over the duck pond
that was Arethusa's fountain, tomorrow, tomorrow.
All of those people and their lucky lives.
I know what I've done, I cannot look beyond.
I treated all of them badly, my three wives.

IV

On the cathedral steps sprinkled by the bells' benediction
like water that blissfully stained the scorching street,
you were not among the small crowd in the sun,
so many in black against the Sicilian heat.
I never entered the shaded church with its pews
facing the tortured altar, but I hoped to find you:
Oh, I did, half-heartedly, but by now it was no use.
The bells meant nothing or the swallows they lifted;
still I felt you were ahead and I was right behind you,
and that you would stop on your shadow and turn your head,
and there in Sicily turn into salt, into fiction.
I don't know the cathedral's name. It's in Syracuse.
I bought a paper in a language I cannot read.
There was nothing in the paper about this. It wasn't news.

V

We never know what memory will do—
my body humming with so much excitement,
I thought my heartbeat sprouted wings and flew
to Syracuse, your harbour, that its flight meant
a return to Sicily and all its sunlit error
where a Greek tanker lay anchored in the blue;
my shadowy treachery, my columned patience
darted through balconies to the gusting area
of the bandstand facing the Bay of the Saracens.
Translucent ghosts, performing without shadows
silhouettes of black actors, shapes on a vase,
their quarrels caught in an oval, while what she does

in those fierce days still beats across my face
like a startled branch or a dove or some other bird's.
My memory's nostrils prick at these odours,
of burnt concrete, or tar, the smell of words
drying like kelp in a rock-pool to a door's
hinges opening like a heart. Gulls rise
like screeching gossips past the hotel windows
and a bosoming wave unbuttons her white bodice.

VI

There never really was a "we" or "ours";
whatever each enjoyed was separate:
a drizzle's drift, the slant of arrowing showers
on a hot road, on roofs, made them elate,
but with a joy defined by separation—
the languor of a glittering afternoon
when a bay's bowl is full of glittering coins,
or a white road is paved by the full moon,
the same delight that separates them joins
without conversion, but close to happiness
in accidental gusts that made the leaves
agree unanimously with one green yes,
yet made a dark division of their lives.
The clouds shone altar-white on moonlit nights;
he was the stubborn sacrificial victim
of his own hopes, like fireflies whose lights
are like false stars that, with the daylight, dim.

VII

There was no "affair," it was all one-sided.
Bats fretted the treetops then pitched like darts
from the pines. At lunch an invisible presence presided
over the wines and salads as, in fits and starts,
a sinuous organ sobbed to the Bay of the Saracens
flecked with gulls' feathers or the sails of yachts,
yet balance and perfection made no sense.
By the open-air table where I sat alone
a flock of chattering girls passed, premature sirens
fleeing like pipers from the sudden thought of a stone.
Emerald ducks paddled and stabbed their bills
in the cool dark well sacred to Arethusa.
I wondered in the inching sun how it was known
to the ferry's horn, the pines, the Bay's azure hills
and the jeering screaming girls that I would lose her
or an accordion's meandering sob and moan
through the coiled, serpentine alleys of Siracusa.

VIII

How come, despite all this, you never mention old age,
you grizzled satyr with your bristling sea urchin beard,
and a head grown almost as white as this page,
as white cedar flowers shake from the *gommier maudit*,
the cursed cedar, like vowels from your pen? Why?
I'll tell you what they think: you're too old to be
shaken by such a lissom young woman, to need her
in spite of your scarred trunk and trembling hand,
your head rustles with thoughts of her like the cedar

in March, you blaze in her praise like a sea-almond,
the crab scrawls your letters then hides them,
certain that she would never understand.
How boring the love of others is, isn't it, Reader?
This page, touched by the sun's declining arc,
sighs with the same whinge, the Sonnets and Petrarch.

IX

What if all this passion is out of proportion to its subject?
An average beauty, magnified to deific, demonic
stature by the fury of intellect,
a flat-faced girl with slanted eyes and a narrow
waist, and a country lilt to her voice,
that she should infect your day to the very marrow,
to hate the common light and its simple joys?
Where does this sickness come from, because it is
sickness, this conversion of the simplest action
to an ordeal, this hatred of simple delight
in others, of benches in the empty park?
Only her suffering will bring you satisfaction,
old man in the dimming world, only joy is the mark
and silence in the stricken streets where no dogs bark.
I watch them accumulating my errors
steadily repeated as the waves as the sea's
decline, and shadows on the high terrace
facing Syracuse; cafés flare in the dark.

X

Why does she precede every journey, waiting by
the side of the road, sometimes, sometimes under
a flowering tree, seated on a culvert, stubbornly
wearing the same dress, as close or far as thunder
curling up a mountain? See the mat of sunlight
under that cedar? There she is! Look how the hedges
above Recanati blaze like a line of verse,
or how the palm or the pine tree blazon their edges
above where she waits in the dusk, lifting no arm
in greeting, her gaze looking through you.
How did she know where I was going, so calm
in her unacknowledging patience, the fringe
of her russet locks as her figure recedes
towards our inevitable meeting? She can singe
my memory in advance, so I go where she leads.

XI

So the moths came, responding to invitations
to my beloved's funeral, she whom I had killed
with my caustic jealousy, my commonplace love-hatred,
my pathetic patience, my impotent impatience,
my infatuation or whatever it's called;
and a cortège of caterpillars too gaily dressed for such
a solemn occasion adding some gaiety to it
and the usual fanning light-hearted butterflies who have never
taken any death seriously, then also,
an anachronistic blackbird in a frock coat and Homburg
representing some ministry, undoubtedly Culture,

then a white guy I didn't know, some *l'autre boug,*
then the usual stooping ecumenical vulture
who pressed his card on me. All of them had known her,
then a patient deputation of worms. All sympathized
but all hoped, like me, that I had outgrown her,
all knew how much her beauty had been prized.

9.

Spanish Series

I

Plod of a hoof in blood-crusted earth.
Clatter of a rivulet over bleached stones.
Black bulls trampling the cape-shade of cork trees,
wind in the high wheat whispering like surf
in Sicily or the first pages of Cervantes.
Two storks on the bell tower in Alcalá.
The boring suffering of love that tires.
Though you change names and countries, España, Italia,
smell your hands, they reek of imagined crimes.
The cypresses writhe in silence, while the oaks, sometimes,
rustle their foliate lyres.

II

A train crosses the scorched plain in one sentence.
In the cork groves shadows rhyme with their sources.
No name except Andalusia would make sense
from the train window of horses and galloping horses.
Echoes and arches of Spain, the word *campagna*
you smuggled from Italy and its fields of sunflowers;
is there a tilde here for Anna or Anya?
Irises stipple the hot square in passing showers,
shadows pause in their capework, ornate balconies rust,
the sunlight of olive oil slowly spreads in saucers
and loves that are hard to break have a sacred crust.

Esperanza, cherished Esperanza!
Your lashes like black moths, like twigs your frail wrists,
your small, cynical mouth with its turned-down answer,
when it laughs, is like a soft stanza
in a ballad by Lorca, your teeth are white stones
in a river-bed, I hear the snorting stallions
of Córdoba in heat, I hear my bones'
castanets, and a rattle of heels like machine guns.

III

The nausea of absence continued as he read
and wrote and read and wrote in the iron-railed
Spanish hotel with its wrought-iron pergolas
in its inside courtyard, at how often he had failed
with women, in a bullfighting town, Mérida,
its ruined amphitheatre ringed with silent olés
for the flourish of his thoughts, for the self-murder
of his pitiable jealousy. Time might deliver
him of his torment, Time that had gnawed at the stone and
eaten its heart. You, my dearest friend, Reader,
its river running through reeds and lights on the river
by the warp of a willow coiled like an ampersand.

IV

Suppose I lived in this town, there would be a fountain,
a tower with two storks, I called them cranes,
and black-haired beauties passing, then again,
I wouldn't be living in a posh hotel; all of Spain's

heart is in this square, its side streets shot
and halved by the August sun. The bullring would be
closed until Sundays, heat
would scorch the park benches, and there would be a lot
of pigeons hopping on cobbles with their pink feet.
I would sit there alone, an old poet
with white thoughts, and you, my *puta*, would be dead
and only half your name would be remembered
because by then you would have lost power
over my sleep, until all that remains
is the fountains' jet. Storks on the bell tower, or cranes.

10.

In Italy

For Paola

I

The day, grey. The mood: slate. Too overcast to swim,
unless a strong sun emerges; which it may.
Our hands, like ants, keep building libraries, storing leaves
and riddling parchment; our books are tombstones, every poem a hymn.
And that honey-natured, gifted Italian girl
gone from the leaves of *Poesia*, gone from the wet stones
of Rimini as the ants keep scribbling, the crabs keep scuttering, and
the tombstones thicken. She was one of the lovely ones,
lovely in laughter, musical in speech,
so gentle in disposition! Vanished like drying sand,
like the fast shadow of the wind on a sunlit beach,
a crab halts and then continues. Like this ant; this hand.

II

He had seemed negligible but her death
afflicted him with wisdom; now he acquired
authority from pain; you could hear his breath
and the littlest gesture he made was profoundly tired.
Maybe that was what she left him, a strange,
angry diffidence beyond his surrender
and a devotion deeper than his work desired,
for a beauty that had seemed so out of range

of the dull cannon thud that would send her
sprawling on the bedroom carpet; more so
than being merely a widower; they were to be married.
Now she lay white as tousled marble, the classical torso
of a goddess whose brief visit delighted earth.

III

For Giuseppe Cicchelero

The pine flung its net to snare the evening swallows
back to its branches, their flight was brief as bats',
the yachts lit up and brought Siracusa close,
a broken music drifted from the ferry boats.
At dusk the soul rocks in its homesickness,
in the orange hour its silhouette is a palm
spiky as a sea urchin against the sky
beginning to pulse with stars, the open psalm
of a huge cloud slowly absorbed its dye.
Swifts practised their archery and the day's fire
roared over Carthage, over Alexandria,
all of the cities were embers in the sun's empire,
and the night in its blindness would choose a
girl with greater vision, Santa Lucia,
patroness of palm and pine tree whose
alphabet was the swallows of Syracuse.

IV

Roads shouldered by enclosing walls with narrow
cobbled tracks for streets, those hill towns with their
stamp-sized squares and a sea pinned by the arrow
of a quivering horizon, with names that never wither
for centuries and shadows that are the dial of time. Light
older than wine and a cloud like a tablecloth
spread for lunch under the leaves. I have come this late
to Italy, but better now, perhaps, than in youth
that is never satisfied, whose joys are treacherous,
while my hair rhymes with those far crests and the bells
of the hilltop towers number my errors,
because we are never where we are, but somewhere else,
even in Italy. This is the bearable truth
of old age; but count your benedictions: those fields
of sunflowers, the torn light on the hills, the haze
of the unheard Adriatic, while the day still hopes
for possibility, cloud shadows racing the slopes.

V

Those hillsides ridged with ramparts and bell towers,
the crests of olives, those wheat-harvested slopes
through glittering aspens, those meadows of sunflowers,
with luncheon napkins like the mitres of popes,
lanes with long shadows, wide open retreats
guarded by leaping cypresses, shade-splashed ochre
walls, then the towns themselves with streets
as close as chain-mail, named after some mediocre
saint, coiling as one road down to the hazed sea.

All of those little ports, all named for saints,
redeem the sadness that was Sicily
and the stupidity of innocence.
It is like Sicilian light but not the same
sun or my shadow, a bitterness like a loss.
Drink of its bitterness to forget her name,
that is the mercy oblivion allows.

VI

The blue windows, the lemon-coloured counterpane,
the knowing that the sea is behind the avenue
with balconies and bicycles, that the gelid traffic
mixes its fumes with coffee-transient interiors,
transient bedsheets, and the transient view
of sea-salted hotels with spiky palms,
in spite of which summer is serious,
since there is inevitably a farewell to arms:
to the storm-haired beauty who will disappear.
The shifted absence of your axis, love
wobbles on your body's pivot, to the carriage's
shudder as it glides past the roofs and beaches
of the Ligurian coast. Things lose their balance
and totter from the small blows of memory.
You wait for revelations, for leaping dolphins,
for nightingales to loosen their knotted throats,
for the bell in the tower to absolve your sins
like the furled sails of the homecoming boats.

VII

As your red hair moved through Leopardi's house,
it was with its modest, flameless fire, Maria.
We toured its rooms in awe of such suffering, whose
stairs constricted its walls, whose climbing aria
was Silvia and solitude; under dark beams,
passing bound volumes in funereal file,
we heard of the great poet's crippled dreams
from our Caravaggio guide and her white smile.
You seemed wrong for the crowd: separate, distinct,
you belonged to the spring-freckled hills outside
Recanati. Your pert, tanned body wrinkled
under its floral print, your look said:
"Why must they feel that love is a great sorrow?
Don't sparrows dart with joy around this house,
though more lugubrious pilgrims come tomorrow?"
Then I looked from the window of his house
and saw, assembled in the little square,
knights ranked to serve the banner of red hair,
their halberds raised, on half a hundred horse.

VIII

Also in Italy I'd never seen anywhere quite
like it—these squares of harvested wheat, panels of
a green crop, maybe corn, tilled hills in rolling light,
dotted with olive and the cypress that I love,
a bleached river-bed and fields of always surprising
sunflowers around Urbino, like nothing I had read,

small hills gently declining then gently rising,
and above the rushing asphalt the window said:
"You have seen Umbria, admired Tuscany,
and gaped at the width of the harbour at Genoa,
now I show you an open secret, do you know any
landscape as lovely as this, do you know a
drive as blest as this one?" I said: "Monterey.
We stopped the car, too, to take in the light,
the breakers, juniper, pine, and the unfolding skies
of the coast. If the grain flung by the sower
in the card brings such astonishment, such a sure
harvest, I have seen them with my own eyes."

IX

Even this far now from that compact, modest hotel,
white walls of summer, tinkle of the ice-cream cart,
baking bicycle path and mineral water bottle,
another beach postcard stamps itself on my heart;
even this far, weeks later, the itch of sand,
the Adriatic sticks to my back, plating it
with greying salt, bringing irascible mothers and
their rubber-bright children and hating it
at first, the rented chairs, while a hundred
identical iron umbrellas emphasize the size
of the holiday coast and the invincible dread
of families, where each shadow is an oasis
and vanilla-coloured girls rub cream on their thighs
in an advertisement Italy, a plastic happiness
that brought actual content. In the cool lobby,

the elderly idle. I was now one of them.
Studying the slow, humped tourists was my only hobby,
racked now by a whimsical bladder and terrible phlegm.

X

I am astonished at the sunflowers spinning
in huge green meadows above the indigo sea,
amazed at their aureate silence, though they sing
with the inaudible hum of the clocks over Recanati.
Do they turn to face the dusk, just as an army
might obey the last orders of a sinking empire,
their wheels stuck in one rut before the small studs
of stars and the fireflies' meandering fire,
then droop like exhausted meteors in soft thuds
to the earth? In our life elsewhere, sunflowers
come singly, but in this coastal province
there can be entire fields of their temporal powers
spread like the cloak of some Renaissance prince,
their banners will wilt, their gold helms fill the void;
they are poems we recite to ourselves, metaphors
of our brief glory, a light we cannot avoid
that was called heaven in Blake's time, but not since.

XI

If all these words were different-coloured pebbles,
with little pools that the blue heron might drink from,
a mosaic sheeted and glazed by the vanishing bubbles

of the shallows, and bannered waves marching to the sea's drum,
if they were more than black marks on white paper,
and sounds that our eyes make upon their meeting,
they would be all yours, since you are the shaper
of the instant's whim, yours is the steady greeting
of the ground dove in the grove, the net that is hurled
over the wobbling stone bed of the inlet,
and yours is the shell in which an ear is curled
or a praying foetus, prophecy and regret.
Here on the blazing instance of an afternoon, the tiring
heart is happy, the hot sea crinkles like tin,
in the tide pools the black rocks are firing
their usual volleys of mullet in their clear basin;
this is the stillness and heat of a secret place,
where what shapes itself in a rock-pool is a girl's face.

XII

For Roberta

Over and over I will praise the light that ranges
over a terra-cotta wall in Naples, in the ungraspable dusk
that makes every corner flare with the lilacs and oranges
of an amateur painter, praise lurid Venice with its disc
dissolving in the Grand Canal when an inaudible
gunshot scatters the pigeons although Roberta says
that their flocks are now an official nuisance and no sibyl
or Doge can save them, no statue with her lifted arm,
or will they settle again and a Canaletto calm
return to the shining lagoon, to Santa Maria della Salute,
dusk rippling the water with accordion strokes,
from a god striking his trident? I hear the widening sound

under the rattle of vaporettos past handiworks
of lace that, as you warp nearer, turn into stone:
turn into stone, cherished one, my carved beauty
who makes drowsing lions yawn and bronze stallions frisk.

11.

Perhaps it exists on only one horizon—
one with windmills and belfries with questioning cranes,
meadows with chattering aspens, a temperate zone,
equestrian statues and water-braiding fountains,
and, when town breaks off and hedges and trees commence,
the exuberant country we see from the train
with hayricks and duck ponds and ravens on a fence
for an alderman's funeral. Deferential rain
falls ceremonially on cafés and cobbles,
umbrellas blossom and a decent haze
glazes the streets where the cathedral wobbles
in its reflection, a drizzle is quiet praise,
and the unshaven priest in his dusty soutane,
protector of Latin and the widowed cypress,
sees how flocks of starlings record the annals
that preserve history in its immortal greyness
and barges pass in stanzas along canals.
This is poetry's weather, this is its true home,
not where palms applaud themselves and sails dance
in mindless delight and gulls race the foam.

12.

The Lost Empire

And then there was no more Empire all of a sudden.
Its victories were air, its dominions dirt:
Burma, Canada, Egypt, Africa, India, the Sudan.
The map that had seeped its stain on a schoolboy's shirt
like red ink on a blotter, battles, long sieges.
Dhows and feluccas, hill stations, outposts, flags
fluttering down in the dusk, their golden aegis
went out with the sun, the last gleam on a great crag,
with tiger-eyed turbaned Sikhs, pennons of the Raj
to a sobbing bugle. I see it all come about
again, the tasselled cortège, the clop of the tossing team
with funeral pom-poms, the sergeant major's shout,
the stamp of boots, then the volley; there is no greater theme
than this chasm-deep surrendering of power
the whited eyes and robes of surrendering hordes,
red tunics, and the great names Sind, Turkistan, Cawnpore,
dust-dervishes and the Saharan silence afterwards.

II

A dragonfly's biplane settles and there, on the map,
the archipelago looks as if a continent fell
and scattered into fragments; from Pointe du Cap
to Moule à Chique, *bois-canot, laurier cannelles*,
canoe-wood, spicy laurel, the wind-churned trees

36

echo the African crests; at night, the stars
are far fishermen's fires, not glittering cities,
Genoa, Milan, London, Madrid, Paris,
but crab-hunters' torches. This small place produces
nothing but beauty: the wind-warped trees, the breakers
on the Dennery cliffs, and the wild light that loosens
a galloping mare on the plain of Vieuxfort make us
merely receiving vessels of each day's grace,
light simplifies us whatever our race or gifts.
I'm content as Kavanagh with his few acres;
for my heart to be torn to shreds like the sea's lace,
to see how its wings catch colour when a gull lifts.

13.

The Spectre of Empire

I

Down the Conradian docks of the rusted port,
by gnarled sea grapes whose plates are caked with grime,
to a salvo of flame trees from the old English fort,
he waits, the white spectre of another time,
or stands, propping the entrance of some hovel
of a rumshop, to slip into the streets
like the bookmark in a nineteenth-century novel,
scuttering from contact as a crab retreats.
He strolls along the waterfront's old stench
to the balcony shade of a store in Soufrière
for the vantage-point of a municipal bench
in the volcanic furnace of its town square.
I just missed him as he darted the other way
in the bobbing crowd disgorging from the ferry
in blue Capri, just as he had fled the bay
of equally blue Campeche and rose-walled Cartagena,
his still elusive silence growing more scary
with every shouted question, because so many were
hurled at him, fleeing last century's crime.

II

Walking the drenched ramparts, tugging his hat-brim,
maintaining his distance on the deaf page,
he cannot hear the insults hurled at him,
bracing for the sputtering brine. An image
more than a man, this white-drill figure
is smoke from a candle or stick of incense
or a mosquito coil, his fame is bigger
than his empire's now, its slow-burning conscience.
Smoke is the guilt of fire, so where he strolls
in Soufrière, in Sumatra, by any clogged basin
where hulks have foundered and garbage-smoke scrolls
its flag, he travels with its sin,
its collapsed mines, its fortunes sieved through bets.
He crosses a cricket field, overrun with stubble
launching a fleet of white, immaculate egrets.

III

The docks are dark and hooded, the warehouses
locked, and his insomnia rages like the moon
above the zinc roofs and spindly palms; he rouses
himself and dresses slowly in his small room:
he walks to the beach, the hills are brooding whales
against them drift the flambeaux and the lanterns
of the crab fishermen, the yachts have furled their sails.
He goes for this long walk when guilt returns;
indifferent to a constellation's Morse,
his resignation no longer sends
out fleets of power, an echo of that force

like dissipating spume on the night sand.
To the revolving beam of the Cyclopic lighthouse
he hears the suction of his soul's death-rattle,
but his is a history without remorse.
He hears the mocking cannonade of battle
from the charging breakers and sees the pluming hordes
of tribesmen galloping down the hills of sand
and hears the old phrase "*Peccavi. I have Sind.*"
Think of the treaties signed by the same one-ringed hand,
think of the width its power could encompass:
"one-seventh of the globe," we learnt in class.
Its promontories, docks, its towers and minarets,
with the power that vanished as dew does from the grass
in the rising dawn of a sun that never sets.

IV

His fingers sticky with rum around a glass,
he can see the scorched square where a saint presides,
and its dry fountain where lizards shoot through grass
and the cathedral's candlelit insides.
In the sunlit bar the woman draws the blinds,
they look like the slitted lids of a lioness
(the yellow sheaves she hides in are his mind's)
the café is quiet, safe from the street's noise,
what he likes now confirms the aftermath
of great events; a tilted sail, a heron
elaborately picking out its path,
a beetle on its back: such things wear on
his concentrated care since the old scale
has been reduced (as are his circumstances).

On the croton bush by the window the tail
of the cat swishes as a dragonfly dances.
A vast and moral idleness stretching before him,
the café's demotic dialogues at its peak hour.
The things he cherishes now are things that bore him,
and how powerlessness contains such power.
The costumes that he wore, and the roles that wore him.

14.

Pastoral

In the mute roar of autumn, in the shrill
treble of the aspens, the basso of the holm-oaks,
in the silvery wandering aria of the Schuylkill,
the poplars choiring with a quillion strokes,
find love for what is not your land, a blazing country
in eastern Pennsylvania with the DVD going
in the rented burgundy Jeep, in the inexhaustible bounty
of fall with the image of Eakins' gentleman rowing
in his slim skiff whenever the trees divide
to reveal a river's serene surprise, flowing
through snow-flecked birches where Indian hunters glide.
The country has caught fire from the single spark
of a prophesying preacher, its embers glowing,
its clouds are smoke in the onrushing dark
a holocaust crackles in this golden oven
in which tribes were consumed, a debt still owing,
while a white country spire insists on heaven.

15.

A London Afternoon

I

Afternoon. Durrants. Either the lift (elevator),
with shudder and rattle, its parenthesis,
or the brown bar with its glum, punctual waiter
and his whatever accent; biscuits and cheeses
with hot, broadening tea with blessing friends.
Summer London outside, guests, porter, taxis,
the consoling clichés you have come back for,
welcomed, but not absorbed, the little ecstasies
of recognition of home, almost, in the polite roar
of traffic towards dusk; here are all the props,
the elaborate breakfasts, kippers, sporting prints,
the ornate lettering on the smallest shops,
the morning papers and the sense of permanence
under every phrase. This is where it must start:
hereditary in each boy (or chap),
the stain that spreads invisibly from the heart,
like the red of Empire in a schoolroom's map.

II

What have these narrow streets, begrimed with age
and greasy with tradition, their knobbly names,
their pizza joints, their betting shops, that black garage,
the ping and rattle of mesmerizing games
on slot machines, to do with that England on each page

of my fifth-form anthology, now that my mind's
an ageing sea remembering its lines,
the scent and symmetry of Wyatt, Surrey?
Spring grass and roiling clouds dapple a county
with lines like a rutted road stuck in the memory
of a skylark's unheard song, a bounty
pungent as clover, the creak of a country cart
in Constable or John Clare. Words clear the page
like a burst of sparrows over a hedge
"but though from court to cottage he depart,
his saint is sure of his unspotted heart"
and the scent of petrol. Why do these lines
lie like barred sunlight on the lawn to cage
the strutting dove? My passing image in the shops, the signs.

16.

In the Village

I came up out of the subway and there were
people standing on the steps as if they knew
something I didn't. This was in the Cold War,
and nuclear fallout. I looked and the whole avenue
was empty, I mean utterly, and I thought,
The birds have abandoned our cities and the plague
of silence multiplies through their arteries, they fought
the war and they lost and there's nothing subtle or vague
in this horrifying vacuum that is New York. I caught
the blare of a loudspeaker repeatedly warning
the last few people, maybe strolling lovers in their walk,
that the world was about to end that morning
on Sixth or Seventh Avenue with no people going to work
in that uncontradicted, horrifying perspective.
It was no way to die, but it's also no way to live.
Well, if we burnt, it was at least New York.

II

Everybody in New York is in a sitcom.
I'm in a Latin American novel, one
in which an egret-haired *viejo* shakes with some
invisible sorrow, some obscene affliction,
and chronicles it secretly, till it shows in his face,
the parenthetical wrinkles confirming his fiction

to his deep embarrassment. Look, it's
just the old story of a heart that won't call it quits
whatever the odds, quixotic. It's just one that'll
break nobody's heart, even if the grizzled colonel
pitches from his steed in a cavalry charge, in a battle
that won't make him a statue. It is the hell
of ordinary, unrequited love. Watch those egrets
trudging the lawn in a dishevelled troop, white banners
trailing forlornly; they are the bleached regrets
of an old man's memoirs, printed stanzas
showing their hinged wings like wide open secrets.

III

Who has removed the typewriter from my desk,
so that I am a musician without his piano
with emptiness ahead as clear and grotesque
as another spring? My veins bud, and I am so
full of poems, a wastebasket of black wire.
The notes outside are visible; sparrows will
line antennae like staves, the way springs were,
but the roofs are cold and the great grey river
where a liner glides, huge as a winter hill,
moves imperceptibly like the accumulating
years. I have no reason to forgive her
for what I brought on myself. I am past hating,
past the longing for Italy where blowing snow
absolves and whitens a kneeling mountain range
outside Milan. Through glass, I am waiting
for the sound of a bird to unhinge the beginning
of spring, but my hands, my work, feel strange

without the rusty music of my machine. No words
for the Arctic liner moving down the Hudson, for the mange
of old snow moulting from the roofs. No poems. No birds.

IV

THE SWEET LIFE CAFÉ

If I fall into a grizzled stillness
sometimes, over the red-chequered tablecloth
outdoors of the Sweet Life Café, when the noise
of Sunday traffic in the Village is soft as a moth
working in storage, it is because of age
which I rarely admit to, or, honestly, even think of.
I have kept the same furies, though my domestic rage
is illogical, diabetic, with no lessening of love
though my hand trembles wildly, but not over this page.
My lust is in great health, but, if it happens
that all my towers shrivel to dribbling sand,
joy will still bend the cane-reeds with my pen's
elation on the road to Vieuxfort with fever-grass
white in the sun, and, as for the sea breaking
in the gap at Praslin, they add up to the grace
I have known and which death will be taking
from my hand on this chequered tablecloth in this good place.

17.

When light fell on the bushes beyond Soufrière,
it was orderly, it named what it fell on—
hog plum and zaboca, dasheen, tannia, and melon,
and between the hills, the orange and vermilion
immortelles that marked the cocoa's boundaries.
We stopped there, driving in prolonged stupor
through perfection framing itself, like the light
that named the town walls of Le Marche, the shore
of the nibbling Adriatic, that made me elate
as a wind-blown chicken hawk, or an eagle's emblem
over L'Aquila, or where a hidden, guttural brook
recited "Piton Flore, Piton Flore," cedar, cypress, and elm
spoke one language, leaves from a trusted book
open at summer. I stopped and listened to them.

18.

The angle at which the late afternoon light
fell across both canvases revealed the coarse impasto
of the paint, a crudity that now showed so late
in life, when I had imagined I would master
portrait and landscape by this time, I'd be seventy-eight
and had done some more than tolerable, I thought,
things, sold, exhibited them, but the scabrous surfaces
were like some dread disease the paint had caught
that suddenly in that hour raked scenes and faces
to nothing, not a style, just a crass confidence—
a thickness, not of skill as in van Gogh or Bacon,
that showed the self revealed for what it is;
the revelation came so quietly. There was no sound
in the studio, only the sea now chafing outside
with disappointment, with numb dissatisfaction—
a truth that went beyond despair or pride.
At least the grief I felt was my own making,
determined to find purity in putrefaction,
still one that cracked the heart and left it aching.

19.

I come out of the studio for blue air
that has no edges, for a sea white with lace,
shaken again by still another failure.
My mirror seems to want some other face.
The usual bristling halt, my joy upset
by some rhetorical passage in the painting,
too crude, too vain, at which the brush went, Stet!
Blood sugar low. Next thing I'll be fainting.
What glares in there now has taken months
to make, drawing and draft and structure that leapt
into belief with faith that youth had once
that it would soar while lesser talents slept.
The elongated figures of an ascetic
straight from El Greco, his skull-echoing face—
well, imitation is its own aesthetic,
less theft than tribute, as they say these days.
The failed canvases
turn their shamed faces to the wall like sins.
A square of sunlight slowly passes
across the studio floor. I envy its patience.

20.

Mist and the spectral peak coming and going,
in the white rain gone completely, so that
at any second now it could start snowing—
the Matterhorn from my window in Zermatt,
snow on the ledges as hedges of bougainvillea
whiten and freak like Queen Anne's lace, the strange
contradictions grow sillier and sillier,
the green hills whiten to an Alpine range
the colour of envy, the stream's cascade is echoing
like an avalanche; this is not absurd;
my craft and my craft's thought make parallels
from every object, the word and the shadow of the word
makes a thing both itself and something else
till we are metaphors and not ourselves
in an empirical language that keeps growing,
associations so astute they frighten
us as in that flash when I saw Petit Piton
for one second with a tingling of the scalp,
a shape that rhymed with its identical alp
till, more than for one instant I, too, whiten.

21.

A Sea-Change

With a change of government the permanent cobalt,
the promises we take with a pinch of salt,
with a change of government the permanent aquamarine,
with a reorganized cabinet the permanent violet,
the permanent lilac over the reef, the permanent flux
of ochre shallows, the torn bunting of the currents
and the receding banners of the breakers.
With a change in government no change in the cricket's chirrup,
the low, comical bellow of the bull, or
the astonishing symmetry of tossing horses.
With a change in government the haze of wide rain
which you begin to hear as the ruler hears the crowd
gathering under the balcony, the leader who has promised
the permanent cobalt of a change of government
with the lilac and violet of his cabinet's change.

22.

May my enemy be assuaged by these waves
because they are beautiful even to his evil,
may the drizzle be a benediction to his heart
even as it is to mine; they say here that the devil
is beating his wife when the sun shines through the wires
of fine, fine rain. It is not my heart that forgives
my enemy his obscene material desires
but the flare of a leaf, the dart of a mottled dove,
the processional surplices of breakers entering the cove
as penitents enter the dome to the lace of an altar;
beauty so shaping neither condemns nor saves
like the tenets of my enemy's church, the basilicas
of tumbling cherubs and agonized saints
and riots of purpureal cloud; though I have cause
I will share the world's beauty with my enemies
even though their greed destroys the innocence
of my Adamic island. My enemy is a serpent
as much as he is in a fresco, and he in all his
scales and venom and glittering head is
part of the island's beauty; he need not repent.

23.

What? You're going to be Superman at seventy-seven?
Got your weight down? Okay. You've lost seven pounds,
but what you've also lost is belief in heaven
as dear friends die. Still making his rounds,
the postman, the scyther, Basil, whatever you call him—
a cyclist silently exercising on Sunday
down a shade-striped avenue of casuarinas
with bursts of foam on the breakwater's wall. I'm
sure everyone knows it will happen one day,
the yachts, nodding agreement in all the marinas,
the blackbirds in frock coats, the frog's staccato hymn,
seven less pounds and you'll need a slimmer coffin.
You suffer from a furious itch that raises welts
on your neck and forearms, so now you swim
early in the morning to avoid the sun; fear melts
before daylight's beauty, despite all that coughing.

24.

The sorrel rump of a mare in the bush,
her neck stretched out in a shuddering whinny
is straight out of Uccello or Marini,
this salt-promised morning on the road to the beach.
A fine mist carries me to other places—
that haze which means it is raining in Monchy,
and perhaps on the cobbled streets of (here memory pauses).
What was that seafront hotel facing Syracuse?
It will come back like her cheekbones, her face's
aboriginal symmetry, it will all come back,
the obsession that I prayed I would lose,
the voice that stirred like a low-tempered cello,
and the esplanade's name … help me, Muse.
Who'd have thought this could happen, the yellow
fading hotel, and now, Christ! her name?
Only the sun on the seafront stays the same
to an old man on a bench for whom the waves are not news.

25.

On Capri

Light frames itself in little squares; a journal.
Past the white terrace the crowd jerks to the prose
of a guidebook; they file from the frescoes:
cardinals, nuncios, infantry captains, the occasional
dwarf, corn-plaited madonnas, assassins (bead-eyes, bumpy nose);
they pour from paintings and bring them up to date
their silent language startled into noise,
as if a bent finger stirred them or a wand
conducted articulate limbs, gave breath and voice
to flaking paint and flexion to each hand
carrying a shopping bag; Mantegna, Crivelli,
the face of a tourist by Andrea del Sarto:
their duty made the commonplace immortal,
and the women, the women! Hard to
see them as that only, that one, for instance,
paused at a shop door in shades, at a glance,
just a tanned girl or Proserpine at spring's portal.

26.

Their numbers do not fade into a page
of last year's diary, but, in dumb addition
stand with addresses like locked doors, in rage
that all our memories confront omission
while their directory builds and a gaping dial
dares you to ring them; they cannot explain
their absences as mixed appointments (nor deny all
that was held in one long breath would contain
them in a gravestone's closed parenthesis).
Numbers like flowers beaten down by rain
or shrivelled by sun until all climate ceases
or the numbers rearrange themselves again.
Sticks loosened from a pile; even the foam
that swirls so lustrously over the sea-stones
vanishes, but numbers keep their forms
and faces we still cherish of the ones
we love, lost, hallowed and reduced
to the echo of the numbers we skim quickly
from a new pain to which we will grow used,
like pebbles to the hoarse, numbering sea.

27.

Sixty Years After

In my wheelchair in the Virgin lounge at Vieuxfort,
I saw, sitting in her own wheelchair, her beauty
hunched like a crumpled flower, the one whom I thought
as the fire of my young life would do her duty
to be golden and beautiful and young forever
even as I aged. She was treble-chinned, old, her devastating
smile was netted in wrinkles, but I felt the fever
briefly returning as we sat there, crippled, hating
time and the lie of general pleasantries.
Small waves still break against the small stone pier
where a boatman left me in the orange peace
of dusk, a half-century ago, maybe happier
being erect, she like a deer in her shyness, I stalking
an impossible consummation; those who knew us
knew we would never be together, at least not walking.
Now the silent knives from the intercom went through us.

28.

The gulls settle like standards on the piles
while pluming waves march past them in their legions;
in the accommodating light, the crescent miles
of Rodney Bay, memory revisits two regions:
one, liquid Venice, then the indigo weight
of solid Stockholm. In both a cherub smiles
at gurgitating, lion-headed fountains, their basins bright
with chattering water, repetitious questions;
one region consonantal, obdurate,
the other vowelled. I pay both allegiance
and gratitude, for light's net that would dance
on the room's walls, the wires, poles, and the freight
of bobbing gondolas and the unknown domes
of palaces and chapels, Santa Maria della Salute
and, in a summer sun, traffic like Stockholm's
white ferries, blinding, bound for the islands.
On a day like this, all blaze with the same beauty.

29.

It is "old Europe" in her voice. The clichés rise
like a flutter of starlings from the wet cobbles,
the years yaw like yachts on the Oder, the eyes
of the lindens tremble and close, bells bless
the railed park where veterans hunch on benches
and widows shoo the goose-stepping pigeons.
In the green canal ducks steer; its stench is
oddly comforting, the sweet reek of moss; two swans
rehearse some opera. In her voice silent bicycles
glide along paths: "We have great woods
in Belgium," while a landscape of leafless sticks is
still all there is of Bear Mountain. Her soft words
float over the sparkling Susquehanna; towns
I cannot pronounce speckle her senses,
a Europe spiked with spires and russet nouns
glimpsed between birches. She grows more beautiful
the more she remembers: her husband at attention
in his white doctor's tunic delivered from the evil
of Stalingrad and Riga, wars not worth mention.

30.

All day I wish I was at Cas-en-Bas,
passing incongruous cactus which grows in the north
in the chasm-deep ruts of the dry season
with the thunderous white horses that dissolve in froth,
and the bush that mimics them with white cotton
to the strengthening smell of kale from the bright
Atlantic, as the road-ruts level and you come upon
a view that dissolves into pure description,
a bay whose arc hints of an infinite
Africa. The trade wind tirelessly frets
the water, combers are long and the swells heave
with weed that smells, a smell nearly rotten
but tolerable soon. Light hurls its nets
over the whitecaps and seagulls grieve
over some common but irreplaceable loss
while a high, disdainful frigate-bird, a *ciseau*,
slides in the clouds then is lost with the forgotten
caravels, privateers, and other frigates
with the changing sails of the sky and a sea so
deep it has lost its stuttering memory of our hates.

31.

My climate now is the marsh, the leaden
silver water that secretes in reeds
or moves with a monody that happily might deaden
endeavour and envy and the waste of noble deeds
for reputation's sake; my frenzy is in stasis,
like a shallop with a staved-in hull.
I fly like the slate heron to desolate places,
to the ribbed wreck that moss makes beautiful,
where the egret spreads its wings lest it totter
on the aimed prow where crabs scrape for a perch,
all that vigour finished with which I sought a
richer life than this half-hearted search.
I am thinking of a specific site
that is Hunter's Cove: away from the road
a frog shoots its tongue at the stars
and traffic; of a marsh in marsh-light
with charging dusk and the boom of a toad
in the reeds at the firefly-flecked night
and a heaven improbably swayed in mirroring water.

32.

Be happy now at Cap, for the simplest joys—
for a line of white egrets prompting the last word,
for the sea's recitation re-entering my head
with questions it erases, cancelling the demonic voice
by which I have recently been possessed; unheard,
it whispers the way the fiend does to a madman
who gibbers to his bloody hands that he was seized
the way the sea swivels in the conch's ear, like the roar
of applause that precedes the actor with increased
doubt to the pitch of paralysed horror
that his prime is past. If it is true
that my gift has withered, that there's little left of it,
if this man is right then there's nothing else to do
but abandon poetry like a woman because you love it
and would not see her hurt, least of all by me;
so walk to the cliff's edge and soar above it,
the jealousy, the spite, the nastiness, with the grace
of a frigate over Barrel of Beef, its rock;
be grateful that you wrote well in this place,
let the torn poems sail from you like a flock
of white egrets in a long last sigh of release.

33.

In Amsterdam

I

The cruise-boats keep gliding along the brown canal
as quiet as prayer, the leaves are packed with peace,
the elegant house-fronts, repetitive and banal
as the hotel brochure, are still as an altarpiece.
We cruised it with Rufus Collins once, a white macaw
on his piratical shoulder. Rufus is gone.
Canals spread reflection, with calm at the core.
I reflect quietly on how soon I will be going.
I want the year 2009 to be as angled with light
as a Dutch interior or an alley by Vermeer,
to accept my enemy's atrabilious spite,
to paint and write well in what could be my last year.

II

Silly to think of a heritage when there isn't much,
though my mother whose surname was Marlin or Van der Mont
took pride in an ancestry she claimed was Dutch.
Now here in Amsterdam, her claim starts to mount.
Legitimate, illegitimate, I want to repaint
these rubicund Flemish faces, even if it's been done
by Frans Hals, by Rubens, by Rembrandt,
the clear grey eyes of Renee, the tree-shade on this side,
the chestnuts that glitter from the breakfast window,
why should I not claim them as fervently as

the pride of Alix Marlin an early widow,
as a creek in the Congo, if her joy was such?
I feel something ending here and something begun
the light strong leaves, the water muttering in Dutch,
the girls going by on bicycles in the sun.

34.

Willows in scratchy lines of a van Gogh drawing,
striped farmyards, bridges, canals, a spray of rooks,
a man in clogs with a barrow, barges at their mooring;
my half-ancestral country in coffee-table books;
and once on a vague visit, windmills and dykes,
skeletal, engraved with a sharp Northern misery
that burst into yellow and madness. I turn pages
for some spasms of heritage, the days when I painted
in the furnace of noon. All that was ages
ago, before I became more acquainted
with love and the suffering that love likes,
the terror of a field with clamorous, cacophonous cawing.

35.

All of this happened when I turned away,
the deliberate delight in incoherence, the whiff of chaos
off the first page of some new book, the putrescent decay
of drawing which I had begun to smell, the coarse
exuberance that passed for wit, it's still incredible the way
my gift abandoned me like a woman I was too old for,
I thought it was the violet that stood up to the armoured car,
I thought it was the wet leather smell of a mare,
I thought it was my voice, my shell-cupped ear,
all of this happened when I turned my head
for just a second from the page. I couldn't hear whose—
either the gift or what it loved was dead,
not just the nightingale's, but the ground dove's coos.

36.

Severance, the thread loosening from the emblem,
the red field throbbing with the arrogance of despair,
boring enigmas, riddles, you have distanced them
from the pain of life, from your task, for the blue air
that persists with happiness that surrounds your naïve
narrative painting, your backward, dated moralizing
on sublime proportion; sand through a sieve.
They force your praise, well no more criticizing
naïve or abstract art, but the one way to live;
facing the high ochre cliffs of Dennery, the white
eternally coming combers, the salt wind, the true.
Wake up again to a dawn trembling with joy,
the silver beads on a dasheen leaf; the dew
of the small morning at Vigie when you were a boy,
a vessel, a trembling branch, a nodding acolyte
with the blackbird, not in the geometry of galleons
of abstract museum openings. Cherish the uninterpreted light
of approaching eighty, let your ignorance increase
as fashion fades, and cities decide what is right.

37.

Quick, quick, before they all die, the hard ebony
head of Arthur Jacobs, the bare pate, the broken teeth
that make his grin more powerful, a man with no money
despite his tremendous presence, light as a leaf
and as delicate dancing, coal-black and like coal
packed with inspiring fire, a diamond with its memory fading;
Jesus, the beauty he contains, a beauty of soul,
no less than that, a wit, an intelligence, the degrading
indifference he has had to endure; some of the best already
gone, Wilbert Holder, Claude Reid, Ermine Wright
against the wind for a long time they kept a steady
flame of devotion, they had to do what was right
for their calling against their most polished detractors
like those who claim they cannot be black and actors,
I mean mean minds who find a contradiction
in their passion and sacrifice, but whom
I cherish more than the most overprized fiction.
I must clear the house of my head, I must make room
for a shrine before they all die, with fireflies and starlight.

38.

On the shore of the mind seaweed accumulates
in the tangling coronals, widowing wreaths; the Atlantic
commotion of Cas-en-Bas heaves, deep-sighed, freights
the clear swell like a lily pond with leaves and thick
stems and the gaps that open onto
ceaselessly charging whitecaps whose spuming crests
are African horsemen; the white shore you are drawn to
is deeper than the tide; if the soul ever rests,
its next beach will be Dakar. Horses whinny
in a grove with mounted tourists, one your granddaughter;
those fields of seaweed reach as far as Guinea.
Gulls beat like sails to cross the severing water
and bones and shells rattle. What weight,
what mass of time is borne by the riding child, what ignorance
of the heaving wreaths, as if this image could expiate
centuries: the horse, the shining girl, the weed-fretted sands!

39.

For the crackle and hiss of the word "August,"
like a low bonfire on a beach, for the wriggling
of white masts in the marina on a Wednesday
after work, I would come back and forget the niggling
complaints of what the island lacks, how it is without
the certainties of cities: for a fisherman walking back
to this village with his jigging rod and a good catch
that blazes like rainbows when he shows it to you,
for the ember that goes out suddenly like a match
when the day and all that it brought is finished,
for the lights on the piers and for the first star
for whom my love of the island has never diminished
but will burn steadily when I am gone, wherever you are,
and for the lion's silhouette of Pigeon Island,
and your cat that presumes the posture of
a sphinx and for the long, empty sand
of your absence, for the word "August," like a moaning dove.

40.

A dun day brightening, clouds like grey flannel,
but, more than the usual, occasional sail,
a grey-hulled tanker anchored in mid-channel,
hazed by the distance and a sunlit drizzle.
They never pause going farther north, or else they seem
to wait until I silently send up a flare
to signal my lifelong distress, wave flailing arms
against such paradisal luck at being stuck here,
among scuttling crabs and the ribbed hulks of palms
looking like frozen detonations, each
ghostly anchored tanker is a young man's dream
of flight, adrift in all the ports of the world
where he has left his name scrawled on a beach,
hiding in ramshackle harbours with a white beard
like a sea urchin, a skin cracked like leather:
that when masts crack and lightning bolts are hurled
he would have seen the world in its worst weather,
quiet as the tanker grazing in midstream.

41.

In memoriam, John Hearne

Whatever the parish, cored in cobalt green,
the breadfruit's broad, open palm, coralita
embroidering the full hedges, St. Elizabeth, Trelawny,
sounding like perpetual spring pouring a litre
of chilled white wine, slopes of raw red dirt,
I think of him now as his own phantom walking
along a cool mountain road with his white panama
and the martial, bristling moustache, his tawny
skin, howling at his own puns, *friend or enema*;
alone on his own road as the car makes a turn
and he is gone, gone without turning his head
to acknowledge our emerald friendship, I mean John Hearne,
his prose rustling from a tall cedar. He heard
his sentences rustle like branches, the hidden
noise of a spring constant under mountain fern
walking straight as a gift that did what it was bidden,
to praise how a horse crosses a meadow, un-ridden,
but purposefully, pausing to whinny and snort,
the sweat sheen on it, deep in remembering thought.

42.

For Lorna Goodison

This prose has the gait of a mule urged up a mountain road,
a slope with wild strawberries; yes, strawberries grow there,
and pines also flourish; native trees from abroad,
and coffee-bush shining in the crisp blue air
fanning the thighs of the mountains. Pernicious ginger
startles around corners and crushed lime
leaves its memory on thumb and third finger;
each page has the freshness of girlhood's time,
when by a meagre brook the white scream
of an egret beats with the same rhythm as crows
circling invisible carrion in their wide dream;
commas sprout like thorn-bush alongside this curved prose
descending into some village named Harvey River
whose fences are Protestant. A fine Presbyterian
drizzle blesses each pen with its wooden steeple over
baking zinc roofs. Adjectives are modestly raised in this terrain;
this side-saddle prose on its way to the dressmaker
passes small fretwork balconies, drying clothes
in a yard fragrant as Monday; this prose
has the sudden smell of a gust of slanted rain
on scorching asphalt from the hazed hills of Jamaica.

43.

Forty Acres

To Barack Obama

Out of the turmoil emerges one emblem, an engraving—
a young Negro at dawn in straw hat and overalls,
an emblem of impossible prophecy: a crowd
dividing like the furrow which a mule has ploughed,
parting for their president; a field of snow-flecked cotton
forty acres wide, of crows with predictable omens
that the young ploughman ignores for his unforgotten
cotton-haired ancestors, while lined on one branch are a tense
court of bespectacled owls and on the field's receding rim
is a gesticulating scarecrow stamping with rage at him
while the small plough continues on this lined page
beyond the moaning ground, the lynching tree, the tornado's black
      vengeance,
and the young ploughman feels the change in his veins, heart, muscles,
      tendons,
till the field lies open like a flag as dawn's sure
light streaks the field and furrows wait for the sower.

44.

"So the world is waiting for Obama," my barber said;
and the old fences in the village street and the flowers
brimming over the rusted zinc fences all acquired
a sheen like a visible sigh, and indoors,
in the small barber-shop, an election poster
joined another showing all the various hairstyles
available to his young black clients that cost the
same no matter who you were—President of the U.S.—
head smooth as a bowling ball my barber smiles
"Is that a Muslim or African name, Obama?"
benign and gentle with his swift-snipping scissors,
"I wish him luck," and luck waits in each
gable-shadowed street that leads to the beach.
Polo loves politics: once in the glass
there were photos of Malcolm, King, Garvey, Frederick Douglass
frowning in the breadfruit window, also
the yapping dogs, the hoses, the church in Alabama.
Polo is young, black, bald under his baseball cap
but more than a barber he is delicate, adept,
and when I leave his throne, shake shorn hair from my lap,
I feel changed, like an election promise that is kept.

45.

In the leathery closeness of the car through canefields
burdened with sweetness under the scudding stars,
I reflect on the bliss of failure, how it yields
no secret, no moral or blame while its suffering stays,
how every corner you christen now conceals a crisis.
On a hill the window-lit abbey of Mount Saint Benedict
passes like a ship in the night as a sickle moon rises
from conspiring, nodding cane and lights a hermit
crouched in his foetal cell as I did with my verses.
You drive towards cries and hugs that will comfort you
while the monk denies himself love that can contradict.
You remember those who supported and those who fought you
were stronger than wood or stone, you built a vision;
the lights of London, its bars, theatres, cathedrals,
that with the glass rolled downward like the night wind
in the canes, the treacherous joy with which a star falls,
mean even less now; what you have left behind
is the tacit pity of the heaven over Saint Paul's,
while from that clover-leaf highway rises
the loving city that takes you back as its son.

46.

Here's what that bastard calls "the emptiness"—
that blue-green ridge with plunging slopes, the blossoms,
like drooping chalices, of the African tulip, the noise
of a smoking torrent—it's his name for when rain comes
down the heights or gusts in sheets across the meadows
of the sea— "the emptiness," the phrase applies
to our pathetic, pompous cities, their fretwork balconies,
their retail stores blasting reggae, either India in the eyes
of uniformed schoolchildren or the emptiness. The image
is from Conrad, of a warship pointlessly firing
into the huge empty jungle; all the endeavours
of our lives are damned to nothing by the tiring
catalogue of a vicious talent that severs
itself from every attachment, a bitterness whose
poison is praised for its virulence. This verse
is part of the emptiness, as is the valley of Santa Cruz,
a genuine benediction as his is a genuine curse.

47.

Epithalamium: The Rainy Season

For Stephanos and Heather

It is coming with the first drops mottling the hot cement,
the patterns budding in the pool, with a horizon
as wide and refreshing as the rain-veiled *Georgics*,
with the upward swoop of the dove, with the heron
quickening its gawky stride; watch a sail
hide her face in mist and the barred sun shrivel
into gathering cumuli, those huge clouds
trawling gauze skirts of rain as camera-flashes
of lightning record the rattling thunder
and the lances of drizzle start marching.
                    But nothing can equal
the surge of another's presence, the separately beloved
whose reign is the rain's, whose weather is the fragrant darkness
of the parlour, in the kitchen, the lightning's cutlery. But O
when the bursting storm rattles the sky's ceiling
and her body draws closer as a vessel warping
into you, her port, her aisle, and she gently rocks,
her ribs brushing yours, O, on your wedding day
may the worried banners of cirrus fade as the storm moves away.

48.

All hallowed, as the stalactites of the Duomo,
the spectral Antarctic of the cathedral, extend the cliché
by an ice cream at La Galleria for whom a
gale-haired beauty pushes a canto in Dante
open like a glass door, the beauty of Beatrice a rumour
here too as in Florence. In transparent summer Milan
is Mediterranean: you expect a butterfly to simmer
on a hydrant, shallows to lap around a traffic island,
and a white sail to cross where the avenue ends.
In the second life I have made so many friends!
Laughter and lemonade among the young poets
sailing into each other's arms like boats into ports
in the Hotel Brunelleschi, I seat them again—
Matteo with the head of an Indian, that jug by Gauguin,
Luigi like a plump burgher, inseparable from
his crammed briefcase, flute-thin Paola, Christina, Patricia,
Vanni, with their own books now; but if there is a form
my muse would take, don't let this hurt her—it is
storm-haired, full-lipped, with axe-blade cheeks: Roberta.

49.

I suppose yes, they should be included,
your work has led to such improbable venues,
these sunsets over Brussels, the flashing windows
of the Grand Hotel and the soft enquiries
of the cocktail piano, "Do you know what you did?"
to the clatter of the crowd at dusk. You acquire more fragments
trying to decipher conversations, posters, menus;
But why, once, instead of a bus you saw
a rock with chattering gulls or your island sky as
it filled with golden wine-light slowly, like your glass?

II

Don't loiter in the neighbourhood of friendship.
The best of them will disappoint, will shut
the door quietly, do not be amazed at your exclusion.
Nothing means as much as their career;
the famous can be grub-like, the towering ones
turn into beetles; do beetles amaze you?
Remember the electric daylight of the emerald hummingbirds
in the bushes, they were like the purity
of first love, they were like the ferocity of innocence
like her brow, damp with a few hairs,
the whole afternoon in her hazel eyes.
Then, after her, the excusable treacheries.

50.

Barcelona

To Robert Antoni

There was a roar outside like a rocket arching
over the roofs this morning, then, under
the black iron balconies, a brass band, marching,
detonated for some saint or labour union,
defending Catalonia with civic thunder.
You smiled down at them with their banners and sashes;
but all you did in Barcelona was cough,
like one of those veterans with mournful moustaches
left over from the Civil War. That is not enough
for such a great city, but you take time in portions,
one cough at a time, your personal thunder
that turns compassionate heads. What I had waited
for was the name to be a banner over every street,
crucifixions on velvet, candles and purple crêpe,
for the crowd in the plaza to leap to its feet
at the flourish and trembling stasis of the matador's cape.
I could never join in the parade; I can't walk fast.
Such is time's ordinance. Lungs that rattle, eyes
that run. Now Barcelona is part of the past.

51.

No opera, no gilded columns, no wine-dark seats,
no Penelope scouring the stalls with delicate glasses,
no practised ecstasy from the tireless tenor, no sweets
and wine at no interval, no altos, no basses
and violins sobbing as one; no opera house,
no museum, no actual theatre, no civic center
—and what else? Only the huge doors of clouds
with the setting disc through which we leave and enter,
only the deafening parks with their jumping crowds,
and the thudding speakers. Only the Government
Buildings down by the wharf, and another cruise ship
big as the capital, all blue glass and cement.
No masterpieces in huge frames to worship.
On such banalities has life been spent
in brightness, and yet there are the days
when every street corner rounds itself into
a sunlit surprise, a painting or a phrase,
canoes drawn up by the market, the harbour's blue,
the barracks. So much to do still, all of it praise.

52.

Elegy

For Aimé Césaire

I sent you, in Martinique, *maître*,
the unfolding letter of a sail, a letter
beyond the lines of blindingly white breakers,
of lace-laden surplices and congregational shale.
I did not send any letter, though it flailed on the wind,
your island is always in the haze of my mind
with the blown-about sea-birds
in their creole clatter of vowels, *maître* among makers,
whom the reef recites when the copper sea-almonds blaze,

beacons to distant Dakar, and the dolphin's acres.

53.

The hulls of white yachts riding the orange water
of the marina at dusk, and, under their bowsprits, the chuckle
of the chain in the stained sea; try to get there
before a green light winks from the mast, the fo'c's'le
blazes with glare, while dusk hangs in suspension
with crosstrees and ropes and lilac-livid sky,
with its beer stein of cloud-froth touched by the sun,
as stars come out to watch the evening die.
In this orange hour the light reads like Dante,
three lines at a time, their symmetrical tension,
quiet bars rippling from the *Paradiso*
as a dinghy writes lines made by the scanty
metre of its oar strokes, and we, so
mesmerized, can barely talk. Happier
than any man now is the one who sits drinking
wine with his lifelong companion under the winking
stars and the steady arc lamp at the end of the pier.

54.

This page is a cloud between whose fraying edges
a headland with mountains appears brokenly
then is hidden again until what emerges
from the now cloudless blue is the grooved sea
and the whole self-naming island, its ochre verges,
its shadow-plunged valleys and a coiled road
threading the fishing villages, the white, silent surges
of combers along the coast, where a line of gulls has arrowed
into the widening harbour of a town with no noise,
its streets growing closer like print you can now read,
two cruise ships, schooners, a tug, ancestral canoes,
as a cloud slowly covers the page and it goes
white again and the book comes to a close.